# Epitaph for the Beloved

*poems by*

# Carol Lynn Stevenson Grellas

*Finishing Line Press*
Georgetown, Kentucky

# Epitaph for the Beloved

Copyright © 2019 by Carol Lynn Stevenson Grellas
ISBN 978-1-63534-956-6  First Edition
All rights reserved under International and Pan-American Copyright Conventions. No part of this book may be reproduced in any manner whatsoever without written permission from the publisher, except in the case of brief quotations embodied in critical articles and reviews.

## ACKNOWLEDGMENTS

*Thick with Conviction:* "Mirror in My Room"; *Communion:* "Unlit Hours"; *The Blue Hour:* "What the Dying Seek"; *Poetry Quarterly:* "Glassdoor"; *The Stray Branch:* "Black Velvet Butterfly"; *Rag Lit Poetry:* "Solicitation to a Tree"; *War, Literature and the Arts:* "Anne Frank's Diary Speaks"; *Ken Again:* "Honeymoon Girl"; *Five Poetry:* "When they Finally Grow Up"; *Chantarelle's Notebook:* "Afterlight/ the Miscarriage," "Babylon," "Child in the Distance; *Memory House University of Chicago:* "An Ode to Sugar Pie," "Wifely Houdini Promise,"; *Hermeneutic Chaos:* "Wild Thing"; *Peacock Journal:* "But I Could Not Save that Dog"; *Sassafras:* "Before the Pink House"; *Wilderness House Literary Review:* "Injured in the Line of Duty," "Womanizer"; *The Tower Journal:* "What You Might Not Know"; *Red Fez:* "Things My Mother Told Me"; *SAC Poetry Center:* "Revelations"; *Scape Goat:* "End to End"; *Shine Journal:* "Call to Mind"; *Triggerfish Critical Review:* "The Saddest Thing"; *Touch, the Journal of Healing:* "There is No Sleep for One Who Prays"; *Ink, Sweat and Tears:* "My Mother at a Job Interview"; *OVS:* "Mouse Queen"; *North West Literary Review:* "Breeched"; *The Milo Review:* "Bad Poem"; *Thick with Conviction:* "At the Molecular Level"; *New Mirage Journal:* "Note from Grover"; *Tipping the Sacred Cow Anthology:* "Sleeping Beauty Betrayed"; *Knot Journal:* "The Night I Lured him to Me"; *Splash of Red:* "A Mall in California"; *Clituature:* "Orchidomania"; *Big River Poetry Review:* "Postscript"; *Foliate Oak:* "Red Cape for Sale"; *Ginokso:* "Calibrating a Childhood Musing"; *Motel 58:* "Unseen"; *Soundzine:* "Detonate"; *Umbrella Factory:* "Insert Current Date and Time"; *Shoots and Vines:* "Saturday Chores"; *Peacock Journal:* "For All the Places We Used to Be," "A Day in the Life"; *Ariadne's Thread:* "The Blue Rosary"; *Memory House:* "Scrutinizing the Nun's Story"; *Gold Wake Press:* "Ode to You," "San Francisco to September"; *Poetry Super Highway:* "Damages"; *Tipton:* "Angie's Garden"; *Hudson View:* "A Few Concessions"; *Decompression:* "Ritual Regarding Nakedness"; *Centrifugal Eye:* "Meet Me in the Countryside"; *The Boston Literary Review:* "The Butterfly Room"; *Tinfoildresses:* "Shopping with My Grandmother"; *Eye to the Telescope:* "Troubleshooting the Sun"

"The Inevitable Life of a Bubble," "A Mall in California," "Candelabra," "Detonate," "Unseen," "Call to Mind" and "A Furniture Hoarder's Confession" were part of an award-winning chapbook from Red Ochre Press, titled, *Before I Go to Sleep.*
"The Ceremony," "Big Girl Talk," "Pheromones," "1963," "Escrow" and "An Orchid's Life," were included in a chapbook from Pudding House Press, titled, *Litany of Finger Prayers.*

Publisher: Leah Maines
Editor: Christen Kincaid
Cover Art: El Hada del Lirio by Luis Ricardo Falero, Wikimedia Commons
Author Photo: McKay Photography
Cover Design: Elizabeth Maines McCleavy

Printed in the USA on acid-free paper.
Order online: www.finishinglinepress.com
                also available on amazon.com

Author inquiries and mail orders:
Finishing Line Press
P. O. Box 1626
Georgetown, Kentucky 40324
U. S. A.

# Table of Contents

# Monday's Child Was Fair of Face

**Mirror in My Room**

In my dreams, we are only
silvered reflections bounded

by frames. Sometimes I shine
my brightness into the grayish

glass, only to find an unnamed
vision waiting beyond the other

side. I rub metallic oxide in swirls;
curved motions until a polished

image becomes clear, until I'm able
to press myself against it, equally

aligned with each, until there's
nothing out of reach but the sound

of whimpering foil rustling between
us, until we vanish into broken light

as we pass through the proof of the other.

## Unlit Hours and a Tiny Room That Remains Shut

Behind a closet door, wooden shelves
warp from heaviness. Three books
closed long ago stand together

like little soldiers guarding a village
from intruders. One never knows
if turning the page might upset

the hush of peace, lost history
pressed shut beneath the cover
of darkness. Half-yellowed

from fading, a little dolly wedges
between for protection; head
slumped from brokenness, one right

shoe lost to darkness somewhere over
the years. I can hear her calling
the names of loved ones through

the keyhole. One day I will answer
her dejectedness. One day I will offer
her my condolences for solitary confinement—

one day I will tell her I'm sorry for deserting
her in the midst of martyrdom. One day
I will replace her missing shoe

when I have the courage to search
the apocalyptic rubble, when I have
the nerve to pry it loose from the dead.

## What the Dying Seek

They said she crept across the drenched
grass; crawled on all fours like a soldier
on a battlefield, or maybe a lunatic in search

of cover, beyond the tree-lined sidewalks
and paved roads, alongside the rows
of homes linked each to each, towards

a safe haven, somewhere past herself.
Yet, there was no shelter, no reprieve
or deliberate assassination in spite

of her attempted escape—that midnight
run branded dementia, with final days
pitied, her failure to find release leaving

her inconsolable until the day she was placed
to rest, where I requested her eyes wide
open, arms uncrossed, hair mussed

and outerwear sullied in homage of her last
pilgrimage, the war she eventually won;
the soul cheating the body where lives

a place unbroken.

## Glassdoor

The last time you visited, I was asleep,
and the moon asked me to roll over,
but I was unaware, and you'd already been
dead for so long. Sometimes darkness

breeds light, and your spirit sneaks
in without ever breaking a thing. Nobody
stirs from a vision like that. Sometimes
I wonder how many pills were placed

in that last concoction you took? I'd like
to hear your answers at the pearly gates.
I'd like to know if it's really a sin
to commit suicide. I'd like to say

I think you were brave, but the next
time you call, I'd like to be awake, the window
wide open waiting for your shadow
drawn against the night, undeniable

no matter how fleeting, like breath on glass.

## The Ceremony

I waited inside the old house—
there was a safeness there among
carpets torn and frayed, an old trunk
holding war uniforms from a war fought
before I was born, sat in the corner,
it hadn't been opened in fifty years.

Everything smelled of rosemary,
and dishes were still piled high
dressed in dinner from the night before.
He walked up the steps in his sacred wear;
you could hear the bells ringing
though he wore no jangling things.

Just a cross hung low and swung
from side to side, like a hypnotist's
tool guiding me into a trance.
It caught the light, made patterns
on the sidewalk's path that led him
nearer, coming close,

as if he'd left the land of Oz
in search of Dorothy. A wizard
bringing hope to a dismal situation.
He held a book with gold paper edging;
ribbons hung like streamers from
pages he'd marked and used many times
before. I wanted to lick them,

see if they tasted like Heaven.

## Black Velvet Butterfly

In the midst of quivering wings,
glass stood between you and the light.
An indeterminable force that tried
to claim your soul, while I, a spectator
in your catastrophe, assumed the metaphoric
bravado like an atheist searching for heaven.

Maybe I was your shepherd to freedom,
your flare through a dark night, bringing
you through your calamity, past
the crowfoot on the veranda, near
the meadow where the trilliums grow,

and still, you hovered as if to say thank you
before you found your path to dreams
and diadems, leaving me empty-handed.

## Saturday at the Chapel

*For Robert, After the drowning*

We stood in disbelief,
Ave Maria resonating through
my ears like a mantra
until I didn't hear anymore,
we held our handkerchiefs high,
white flags, signaling to heaven.

I glanced from left to right
as if driving before turns
on the road. No one spoke,
but hands became a human
chain impenetrable
in times of sorrow.

I felt the ecstasy of being risen
as they recounted his walk
to the sea. I decided a divine force
was with him, guiding him in,
pulling him under.

His casket was covered
with a pearl shroud encasing
it like a holy veil of love,
the scent of sacred oil surrounded me,
my head was lit with incense
billowing over, lulling me there.

I was with him for only a minute,
I knew his weightlessness, and he
breathed with me, in and out
my lungs became home to another
force, for only an instant, but I felt
it, his peace with death, and the presence
of a greater power.

## Solicitation of a Tree

Are you the kind of tree a boy can climb
or build a fort of twigs? Do you know
I have a fondness for shade in the summer,
but only when the sun is robed in full
regalia, blistering with heat, the wind losing
itself to a stifling hand that holds back
the wild and rambling delta breeze.

Are you the kind of tree a girl might
engrave initials? Do you have the trunk
for lettering inscribed? Some trees
are soft and forgiving, too malleable
for the edge of a knife, they slough
off their skin and peel like an onion.
I need a tree with a jagged exterior,
one whose stalk is hearty and firm.
A name gets roots in a tree like that.

Are you the kind of tree that teases
a swing. Will you carry long ropes
of twine all the way to heaven?
I need a tree to reach eternity,
raising me up then bringing me
home again. I need a tree that cuts
through clouds, a dependable kind
of tree for being suspended midway
and enabling the fluctuation of motion
forgiving as legs pump the sky.

Are you the kind of tree that shelters
a grave? Do you have a pillowed
place beneath your leaves for a body
to lie down and nestle without
the worry of bending or swaying
from all upheavals left undone? I need
a tree for the afterlife, one that
promises a branch of fruit or acorns

ever ripened and brown. I need a tree
that lives after it dies, that never leans
one way or the other, that stands
erect, even when the world appears
upside-down.

Are you the kind of tree that reads
a poem? Will you recite the words
of the moonlight, the images of rivers
beneath you, and the feeling of wings
fingering through your limbs? Are you
the kind of tree that knows you're more
than a tree, the hum of everything,
a symbiosis, a dwelling to hide in when
the world isn't working, and all you can
rely on is the earth's synergy,
and the splendor of a tree.

## Imaginings

Sometimes I watch myself
through a window, outside
in, the way you can gaze
through and see your image
in glass; a backdrop of greenery
filling the empty space.
My arms and legs covered
in leaves, ripples of light
peering through the lace
of dogwood trees.
There was a day I cried by
a window, before my mother
died, a day I opened a window
wide, to hear someone screaming,
a day I watched an ambulance
take my father away, a day
I smashed a fly with my bare hand,
a day I used my finger to outline
the figure eight on breath, a day
a window saved me with its beauty,
and a day I wanted to break it,
just to find out if I would still
exist without my own reflection.

## Diary of Perpetuity

In the weird energy
of yesterday and now,

the otherworldliness
of tomorrow; signifying

the enigmatic amid
this plane of here and there,

while the moon continues
to display faceless shades

in sugar-white, and light
reactivates our language

within these hidden hours,
moving through a world

like balsa wood rafts
drifting out to sea

and finding our way home
again, in the suppleness

of scars always healing.
While germanium petals

weep their dew; clustered
blooms lean towards tomorrow's

unceasing sun. No flower's
imprint will ever be as beautiful

as that which hollowed its truth.

## A Furniture Hoarder's Confession

It's hard to say why a bare room makes me weep—
the sight of vacant floors and windows stripped
or drape-less. The unoccupied space and reminder
of moving one too many times with unscrewed
bed-frames and the endless setups from place
to place; the opposite of a vagabond, my shopping
cart is full of kitchen sinks and countless pillows
in silk brocade, my grandmother's piano seat
where she lounged on Christmas eve, the étagère
with beveled glass and Ange's maple leaf cups,
the French provincial breakfront with its homey
touch that crowds the birdcage with no apologies,
though the parrot hasn't complained.
There are the high back chairs, the leather
ottoman below the stairs, where I've sat a thousand
times and sipped my cognac from its Waterford
tulip glass, the Persian rug with fringe frayed
from careless vacuuming with company arriving
any minute. Oh you could say it's overdone
that less is more, and I need to Feng Shui
myself into open space through long hallways devoid
of perfectly made benches flanked against
wainscoted walls where pictures hang in gallery
style order, row after row that require straightening
immeasurable times a day, but I'd say more is more,
cram me in tight like Tutankhamun with glints
of gold, and pots that hold macramé plants swinging
from chandeliers, canopies braided from an apex
in the ceiling hanging over me like fast moving
clouds below each corner, saving a cubicle for something
more special than before, if only to me,
where every night I can sleep and dream
of a turquoise settee, sitting tête-à-tête
with you, while I hold down the fort with an eye
for design, a heart formed by loss, so we
might be trapped here forever, locked
in our labyrinth of ageless stuff, as close as sardines.

# Tuesday's Child Was Full of Grace

**Anne Frank's Diary Speaks**

For she marked the date June
12, 1942, her miniscule habitat
in lieu of dying. But you will only know

the parchment of her skin, the broken
and fragmented days between
heaven, hate and back again—

those far-reaching matters of genocide
that seized her thin frame and glowing
heart. I knew her well, long years together

and apart enduring the horrors of war.
Her vellum soul inked, bookcase
yellowed, soft voice unforgotten

as it bellowed silent from the annex;
an underground love like a hidden
weapon stored in the labyrinth

of hollows, hollows, hollows.
Dear sanctuary girl, sanctuary girl,
her tattooed story etched on checkerboard

tome—words held secret withstanding
parades of Holocaust angled crosses,
clockwise bent, swastikas pacing

murky streets, sweet penned being
denying death, her hand unrelenting,
extraordinary child, beautifully wild

unstoppable thing, despite how she wept,
how she wept, how she wept, where
no consequence could thwart memories

divinely kept. Oh, Anne, you're alive

in your letters, chronicled from home through
the house beyond bones, empty shoes

and body piles. Your entries robbed
cloud high still unwritten, lost cries
from a visceral place. Goodness diarized

past your nameless betrayer; coward Nazi
from an ominous space, anonymous,
anonymous, anonymous.

**Big Girl Talk**

She comes to me,
says she needs to write a poem,
speaks of vaqueros and Mexican girls crying,
how the rain sounds through her window,
the color of adobe bricks and missions with graveyards
where the Padres prayed to God under bohemian moons.

I tell her that's beautiful,
ask her to explain what it means,
turn my head as she reads it aloud one more time
because I've lost the will to be even-tempered.
Holding back is an impossible task
I've little need to diminish the cure she's become,

the healer for all that ails as sadness is always inevitable.
She throws her Raggedy-Anne arms around me,
releasing the scent of peanut butter and jelly
like a tonic water targeting every ache I own.
She speaks of southwestern cowboys, love, and beauty.
She is a gift of everything I could have been
wrapped in forgiveness.

## Honeymoon Girl

Ballerina-bloom, as you lie inside my palm
barely opened, tiny little bud, one baby flower,

your perfect nudeness
the scent of strawberries
in your hair, as you lean
against me, shifting

soft flesh from left to right, clinging to my skin,
tight, a baby sundew, drinking nourishment like soup,

I remember you, deep within
my belly, calling my name—
announcing your arrival
with long months of hidden

hiccups and tippy-toe-dancing. That night in Venice,
a peach Bellini seducing the candlelight to a tawny

glow, the window's veil, a cadenced
strum, one thousand
castanets on glass.
He wore an august smile,
and it was the beginning of us.

## When They Finally Grow Up

When they finally grow up and fold up
their childhood in cardboard boxes

in the trunk of their car, leaving a handful
toys on the crook of your chair… the chair

used for rocking through every midnight fever
when moons looked more ominous rather

than white. When you're only remembering
their dreams and delusions and the first time

you held them close to your breast, the way
their hands smelled of water and starlight,

and the endless worry that mothering brings.
When they finally grow up and say they are

leaving, whispering goodbye to their home
and to you, beds unmade in the usual fashion,

closets all mussed, hangers broken in two,
one row of shoes left deep in the attic

that protected the feet of baby-pink skin—
their belongings and drawers chocked full

of memories, crumpled report cards,
and ten thousand promises you know they won't

keep, they'll look back a moment saying, *please
don't worry,* and you'll try so hard to make it all work,

with the door nearly closed on the years
that you've raised them, penciled charts tacked

or glued on the wall… you'll pretend you're not

shocked that your house has an echo

while whispering goodbye as you hug
them, and smile, and thank God for it all.

## What I Told Her

*To My Daughter Who Said, I Once Looked Like Her*

I tell her, you are more striking
than I ever was, the world will be
your oyster, there isn't always

light at the end of the tunnel,
now and then there's just another train,
and sometimes life is bullshit.

I miss my mother, I miss my father
too, and I miss you already. I've made mistakes
you'll never know, a secret is as a secret does,

don't take crap from anyone, to err is human
to forgive divine. My mother slapped
me for letting the nurse push

a feeding tube down her throat. No
good deed goes unpunished; there's
more than meets the eye. Soon

you'll have a stack of boxes that clutter
about your closet floor; souvenirs of those
who've gone before—someday you'll do

something I'll ask you not to do. My mother
said I took her hope away, but hope
is a good breakfast, cross my heart

and hope to die as if hope could ever
lie. Don't forget, I love you.

## What Little Girls are Made Of

Sometime between salad
and passing the vegetables
my daughter told me about

the girls on the softball
team in seventh grade,
how they wore their jerseys

to school. How one of their
teammates lost her battle
with cancer, so all the players

cut their hair and dressed
in uniforms to attend the funeral
that afternoon. She said

it made her sad, and she'd like
to learn to play softball, be part
of a team who loved someone

like that.

## They Were All I Could See; My Road Home.

My tailbone split when they were
born; the back-break of labor.
Some will say it's not a job

for the faint of heart, but I
say a thank you prayer full
of gratitude when I hear

their names. This is a mother's
offering, from a dossier of nights
where each life became my light

in the tunnel, a path to a higher
ground where once was a smear
of tears on shadows. Where they've

been my barometer when directions
to heaven could not be found. Their skin
to skin glory, created by a moonlit

miracle, minus requests for anything
more than a chance to sing a lullaby
or hold a baby close with unseen wings.

Daughters will know their mother's
secret for there's no feigning
something so vast, once arms

are full, and they gaze down at last
to see the grace of God in the face
of the tiniest beautiful being.

## On the Passing of Her Child

*Yes,* I say, *I see it too,* his reflection
beyond the double-pane window. She tugs
my hand and squeezes it tight. *It's going to be
alright,* I say, the prongs in my ring
poking through to bone.

*He's here,* she says, *he's inside now,*
and carries on as I give up trying to understand
the words, listening to the hum of her voice,
the modulation; a primal moan, strange
but happy too.

Her eyes are blue; they're almost wet
like dew in the early morning. She
pulls me close and begins to weep. The
creep of wisteria giving a purple hue
to the sunlight's dance of shadows.

I lean in and say *I hear him too,* his breath
a gust of a dream brushing by my face.
I do my best to trace the outline of a shadow
only to watch her vacant stare as if he was
once there only to vanish through

some invisible door. My palm, all the while
pressed to hers; our hands tied by grip
of fingers, jolts an ache like throbbing
through my core, and I'm not sure
whose pulse is whose anymore.

## Playing Woodwinds to an Unborn or Just Reincarnation

When the lost child is listening for the mother,
he hears her crying through a downpour

of silver keys that rise above the land
unlocking just one door, yet no one's

near enough to answer. Before
the benediction, there was love

soft as the bougainvillea, beyond the gale
of yesteryears forever unknown.

She prays he'll wait till wings have risen
from the ground, past the twinkling of ancient

bars that scrape the latch of forgotten entries.

## Elegy for Kathy

They say you were a child misunderstood
by those who flaunted love yet never could
access the secrets that you kept, the evenings

gone to hours where you wept alone, a darling
save the rumors whispered past your ear
forgotten on the day they came to offer

tribute to your soul. A role they cherished
since enigmas were so daunting in their eyes.
How they tiptoed past your coffin sheepishly

bogus allies never crooning once your name;
unvalued beauty, complex yet troubled
by approval for approval's sake,

you overlooked their callousness through
years of sunless hours until the doublethink
infected every single nuance you possessed

and still, I ponder how we laughed outside
the summerhouse, where we ran inside
because of rain, the way your pinafore displayed

a little brooch against your breast, one silvered
saint your father pinned, a trinket you would wear,
as if he knew an angel might be needed

on your journey there.

## Afterlight/ the Miscarriage

She remembers lullabies, once
upon a time and desires goodness,

a cross hanging god. Gone are the days
she ate scones for breakfast, drank

afternoon tea, overlooking the universe
blighted by stars. She will forget

about breath, her unmoving belly,
undeniable stillness through birth

cord to love. One drop of redness,
her stomach cut open, a life lost

to stardust, the small death of birds.

## Unseen

The black hawks circle above my home;
wings tipped with aerodynamic ease
in a bull's-eye-spin, hunting their sunrise victim.
They slipstream through cloudless blue
like wind-kites surfing the heavens.

My sightless dog waits for breakfast
in chilled air, outside on a bed of iced grass,
while I grind beans in my Betty Crocker
kitchen. The spigot lifted, hot water spills
in waves over sleepy hands, and I hear him
whimper on the lawn, frozen with dew.

*His paws must be numb by now—*

frosty droplets thawing on long blades of green.
The black hawks fly while the dog paces,
as I dabble with contraptions and gadgets,
brewing a perfect pot of house blend.
I'm dressed in a lavender gown,
my feet furred with slippers.
*His paws must be numb by now—*

This is what it's like to be cruel.

**An Ode to Sugar Pie**

Because she is a feathered thing,
I hold her in my upturned hand,

and yet she never tries to fly
though she spreads her wings—

and croons *I love you* every time
I pass her by. There are days

she cries for the wild hollows
of a tree, a cacophony that breaks

my heart. Those days she's like a child,
I take her in my palm and make a home

inside my skin. I cradle her
in a silent benediction

since we both know there's something
greater past the window's ledge

beyond this place called home.
And yet I've robbed her of the rain

the verdant grasslands in the spring,
those days I hold her near and

whisper gently through her unlocked
cage, "forgive me for this crime.

I've made your kingdom small,
and even though you sing you are

a captured soul, the cruelest thing."

## Wild Thing

Forgive me for ignoring
the barking dog lost in darkness
begging for his meal of scraps

and bones, making
his way through garbage
in a dimness only known

to those who've lived
beneath a moon of loneliness.
A moon that shines

its coppery beam as bright
as pennies inside the loafers
I once paraded in fourth

grade. A moon so keen
its sliver of gold
carves through clouds

like an electric searchlight
with a taunting beam
that's flashed my name.

I am a drifter, semi-
unconscious, imagining
hope from an unseen source.

Dog, I am sorry
that you have gone hungry.
I have been a glutinous fool.

## But I Could Not Save That Dog

As we crossed the bridge,
I saw him race the highway's divide

skirting the cars, avoiding the snag
of something sharp, unknowing

he moved like a deer searching
for the meadowlands—

but I could not save that dog,

Though I tried to reach beyond
my window calling him back

as if some lunatic thought entered
his mind, and he embraced it

took the chance, like an untamed thing
craving the badlands. He lost his place

in the world making way for a lark,
or maybe an oasis where another lost dog

awaits the one who's always running.

# Wednesday's Child Was Full of Woe

## Before the Pink House and You Went Missing

I miss the days with two plates of eggs;
scrambled and warm, your face pressed

to mine like a picture captured through glass
beside the window's ledge, the hedge

where bees would swarm around jasmine
potted jardinières that lined our home

on Lancaster Street. Where we would walk
with shadows ignoring the coarseness

beneath our feet like barefoot nomads—
yours, one step ahead of mine, so carefully

avoiding this unbearable existence of following.

## Darling Mother

Darling mother, your only sin
was in leaving, how you stole

half of me into dying until my heart
became unwell, my whole self

in lasting disarray, while you slept
your way to death unaware

of my greatest weeping. Your voice
forever silenced, my biblical display;

a feat so spectacular I became
a human candle, wicking myself up

to a holy place as though fate could be
upturned with enduring supplication.

I offered my soul through your bedroom's
basilica; the orchids limp beside you

I waited for your final goodbye
as though you'd announce your departure—

the good girl I am, this other side
of heaven, unbearable without you.

## Injured in the Line of Duty/ A Mother's Thoughts

In the darkness, my arms are the branches
of a tree that used to cradle you in the storm.
But here in the daylight, I am drunk on sadness
and lost to the thought that time is fragmented,

a prayer broken, interrupted by chance.
I was dreaming about you before
you were born, and then god made you real.
There is something tragic about knowing

your ending is inevitable. If I were a bible
I would fold myself back to your favorite page,
I'd wait by your bedtable. I'd live in the ribbons
dangle over the unread. There are things

children don't know about their mothers,
old stories never shared. But all love
is based on trust, either in yourself
or someone else. Let's not discuss

the meaning of anything unless
we're willing to be accountable. Let's "be
what we pretend to be." Socrates said that.
My mother did too, but she was just

an illusion.

## What You Might Not Know

What you might not know
is that when your mother
dies in her own home,

when she takes her last breath,
and a tear rolls down everyone's
cheek, even hers,

and you are still squeezing
her limp fingers, kneeling beside her,
your face pressed against the coolness

of her pearl white gown, her chest
unmoving...what you might not know
is that your next call will be to the morgue,

and you'll be the one directing them
through the family hallway on the way
to infinity with their steel gurney and white

sheets, while her nurse will be throwing
out unused morphine and a half-filled
urine bag. And someone will call

your name from the other end
of the house, asking you to leave the room,
but all you can do is wait there quietly

as if she really needs you, as if having
your company is better than being
alone, as if one of you might still

know the difference.

## Things My Mother Told Me

*It's bad luck to put a hat on the bed*
No fedora he owned could bring a bend of fate
or anything named unsacred. Although once it landed
firmly between my desire for love and this year's forget-
me-not promises; like a cataclysmic wind that whirls
against a half-opened door, my fingers still holding the feather.

*If you dream of fish: someone you know is pregnant*
One morning I woke with a craving like never before,
my belly greedy with yearning; the taste of salmon
on my tongue, and I knew wisdom was living within me;
all the world's knowledge imprisoned and asleep
in my virgin womb.

*A white moth entering your house means death*
Unless you're able to grasp the light in your palm,
wings unbroken, fingers blending to camouflage
as if you're one with another, then the end is near.
She told me to speak the language of butterflies,
become the essence of radiance; a paralyzing moment
that makes celestial navigation an impossible flight.

*A swan's feather sewn into your husband's pillow will ensure fidelity*
Even the gentlest prick on the head from such a tiny quill
should serve as a reminder you won't stand for much.
Sometimes I dish up waterweed for dinner. It tucks nicely
between my lover's teeth dissuading synchronized swimming
or any wintering near available estuaries.

*Place a hand in front of your mouth before sneezing,*
*or your soul will escape*
Once on a calm night when the moon's reflection
bounced off the window, and all the stars broke
through glass in a fractured light, I saw an image
who used to be me; a mirror from heaven—
or was it me looking back, seeing someone else?
I can't be sure, and I sneeze every time I've come

close to knowing.

*Turning counterclockwise while holding a magnifying*
*glass proves you've told the truth*
This will make you dizzy unless you're chewing a dandelion
sprig, chanting made-up facts. Then a witch named Delilah
will enter your home and cut off your hair for lying. Okay,
I made this one up, but a white moth just entered my house,
I'm not a virgin anymore, there's a black hat on my bed,
I mistakenly used a duck's feather on my husband's pillow,
I buried my heart when my mother died.

## Consider the Mother

What you have heard is true.
There was a diary in her drawer
with leaves bent on inconvenient

pages; words from a suffering heart—
a child waking in a pasture of flowers
bending over bleeding grass;

there were the tears of trees through
a vessel tomb, a womb unmeant
for breathing. Someone brought

a cup of tea, bathed her feet
with iodine, pinned her hair away
from ghostlike skin. The say she smiled

before her cervix curved to dying.
There was the mention of a hanger
and knitting needle; one tiny sweater

crocheted and folded, unknowing
evidence, right next to the bed.

## Memories of Warmth

In the splendor of darkness over
long weeping grass, I see my mother
bend beside a bed of irises

to touch the violet petals. Stem to stem
they blend together unaware a blossom
dies when pulled and tied by twine.

She was never mine to lose, but it
was easy to pretend those days would
linger like unending songs, and when

the loneliness creeps in, I remember jasmine
scented tea and little tangerines we quarter
sliced at three, accompanied with petite

fours for two. Those days we savored minutes
towards the hours of every clock while hands
were holding only happiness, a hollowed stalk.

I remember flowers as my mother
sipped the stars that gathered from a concave
cup the way a griever shows the face of death

before the dying eve. Dawn is breaking,
and she whispers it must be time
for me to leave.

## Revelations

It will be me who'll follow,
*A-tisket a-tasket a green and yellow basket,*
with my wheelbarrow of celluloids,
of Sunday memories, when I was ten.

I'll fold your French gowns tight like origami paper,
*I wrote a letter to my love, and on the way, I dropped it,*
so black spiders won't slip
between damp lace stored in the cellar.

I'll remember the old film,
*I dropped it, I dropped it and on the way I dropped it,*
still locked in cameras you once owned
promising immortality, what a biting lie.

I fear I've done an injustice to you mother,
*A little boy picked it up and put it in his pocket,*
I finally found the dress you asked to be
buried in, yesterday, tucked in an old shoe box.

I broke my promise, forgive me
*A-tisket a-tasket he took my yellow basket,*
and if he doesn't bring it back
I think that I shall die.

## 1963

Though my mother would do her best
posing near our pink Frigidaire
for hours looking beautiful awaiting
her next photo shoot; a leopard demanding
awe from every viewer for its spectacular
gift of gorgeousness, it was my father
who drew sketches of Arabian horses
and danced the mambo in our living room
making daydreams come to life.

He could never be defined by simple adjectives
in the everyday vernacular,
as he was born with an intangible
quality catching the sun with his laughter
so full of fervor, a rousing stirred
from within.  He glowed chartreuse
under the stars, and when light
swept the day he was the essence of heaven—

Every moment was a godly viewing
like surfers on the seventh wave,
hanging ten through the curl.
How I yearned to follow in his wake
sensing the ride that delighted him so,
rejuvenating life with his well
of inspiration day after day.
He was an enigma from the earliest
I recall, a whirling sorcerer of magic.
I was certain he was some kind of saint

reborn in human form, never to be divulged
to any living soul until the day he'd astonish
us all, revealing his wings, spilling beneath
the hem of a pair of trousers, embroidered

with gold trim. He'd give a little flourish
with a crystal staff, and off we'd fly
to paradise together. I still can't believe
he left without me.

**End-to-End**

With the room lit in midday light
and your basket of thread settled

just right, near your fuchsia
painted toes, the bright, haloed

white over your patient eyes,
black lashes fanning up and down

like long spinnerets winnowing
Shalimar across your cheek,

we'd sit side by side on that gold
settee, you threading silk through

needles, basting hems together
again, and again, soft as healing

prayers over a rosary while
you looped each stitch round

and about in repetitive order, blessing
our clothes with a kind of curing

through the darning of holes,
repairing of pockets, as if mending

edges could hold all wishes
through each day's wear. Now

you're not there, and my knees
poke through these fraying seams

while I bow to prayer, though I try
to remember how end-to-end

things always break from too

much weight. This is the way

of an open wound; what dying
brings; unavoidable fate.

## Mothers

Mothers have the joy of holding a child
against their breast, beneath a moon full
of milk-colored light. They lull and woo soft

whispers over the babe that melts inside
the nestling of arms supple as petals brushed
with sun. Mothers know the secrets of infants,

they study the sound of sadness, the subtle
twitch before whining begins then bursts
beyond weeping, like a begonia's eruption

from bloom to withering after it's plucked
from the wild. Mothers have the joy of holding
a child from year to year until there's no longer

fear of the space called leaving, until youth
meets the promise of prayers and the desire
of seeking that which may not be found

in the arms of their mother.

## Call to Mind

I told her we were there last week;
had Greek coffee in her kitchen,

she was dressed in black again
just like she has for forty years.

We checked the closets,
searched for ghosts, and told the nurse

her favorite channels, both of us
covered in a patchwork quilt

with the heater cranked to ninety.
She squeezed my hand extra hard;

pressed it like a piece of fruit,
kissed my face on either side

then twice as we were leaving.
She said she had forgotten that

wondered if we'd be there soon,
I could have told her anything

as long as I said, yes.

## Caterpillar Prayers

You were a butterfly
in the meadow

where no viewer
could see your grace

save the birdlike seraph
perched on a nearby

magnolia leaf; a lingering
nobody awaiting

beauty haloed golden
within the sun's rays.

Your pending explosion
through moonlight eclipsing—

the story you left behind.
My wing snagged on a broken

twig as I tried to follow,
halted without you

stuck between what seems
eternal, like an instar

amid the need of change.
Without you—I am

not the same.

## The Saddest Thing

The saddest thing I've ever seen was a child's tiara resting
on a weather-worn tombstone. The afternoons
when it would rain I'd make my way to the cemetery

just to see how it fared among the dappled leaves
and windblown things of winter.
I found myself remembering her name

during conversations with other women. They'd mention
their children, and I'd think of that little girl and the way
a shimmering crown stayed affixed without the use of pins,

how even the rainiest day couldn't remove an arc
of light from above her head, her row of stars embedded
where I imagined once, the softest flaxen hair.

The saddest thing I've ever seen was the look on someone's
face when they knew I was going to report bad news.
The way they turned this way and that hoping I wouldn't

care about the hollowness in their eyes, as if I expected
something thoughtful to ricochet back from them to me,
propelling us both to a better place. There's a kind

of arrogance in saying it's going to be fine, or maybe
an impassive grace. I've left a penny in one spot a few hours
at a time hoping I'd return to find it. A good omen if so, proving

chance can be planned wherever you go. I keep a buggy
full of dolls beside my fax machine though the wheels
have lost their spin, a small pram that can't be moved carrying

porcelain babies, each with a bow under her chin
who never weep despite the lockdown on a bed of blue. "Don't cry,"
they say, bonnets all tied, tiny darlings from years gone by.

The saddest thing I've ever seen was the way those dolls stared

when I ignored their unblinking eyes. "Don't cry," they'd say
with hair long mussed, to the sound of a letterpress disrupting
their sleep.

"Don't cry," they'd say with no one to hold them, wearing
tattered clothes from their bedded cave. "Don't cry," they'd say
when that tiara fell, one January morning, beside my mother's grave.

## There is No Sleep for One Who Prays

The night you slept with a tube in your throat
I begged the nurse to let me stay
so they placed a cot beside you as if that might
promote an hour's worth of rest, but there's no
sleep for one who prays and I tried so hard
to listen for an answer; some sign that you'd be
alright. I made promises for all failures
and mistakes throughout my life, as though I'd
be repaid in exchange for your wellbeing.

Even the windows felt clouded through smears
of dampness marking glass with reminders
as if some external force was joining in. I could
almost smell the scent of winter circling
your frail face; old memories pushing through
doors locked from outside in proving being lost
is never about where you're going, but knowing
where you've been.

You dozed with an unconscious stare, cold
like rivers in December and I told you stories
of growing up as if you didn't remember years
spent brushing my hair, tying pinafores around
my waist, as if my whole childhood had been
a waste, long forgotten, and when I leaned
over your face to an unfamiliar reserve
I knew no healing could change the outcome,
you were already unwavering in your desire
to leave. And when you put my hand
in yours, I thought a miracle had begun

as if you were coming back to me. I pressed
your fingers to my cheek, pretending you were
loving me again when you were only begging
that I'd pull the tube from your throat. I never
spoke of it; even now that illusion of truth
plagues my days, for refusing your last

request. How I defiantly called the nurse
to adjust the hose resting precariously
on your chest, how it ignited some tiny light
within you to see me gloat with disobedience,
and how for one moment I almost enjoyed
you being angry with me again.

## My Mother at a Job Interview

Let's see...
You've expertise with poison ivy
when your children woke with eyelids
swollen shut and lips that quivered
Mommy, in voices whistle-shrill—

the skill of sitting up each endless
night distracting them from itchiness,
no pill could ever do all that.
The way you rubbed them down

with alcohol when fevers reached
1.4 like some magic Queen of voodoo;
you're a sorceress with more
than wonder hidden in your bag

of tricks, but they will never know
the way you've kept ten thousand
tears inside, alleviating fears,
while praying for those miracles—

so far none denied; as if you knew
they'd always come. How do we
evaluate the sum of all you've done
for them? I think we'll mark

your application, and use a scale
from one to ten, determining
what job you're suited for, till then
how 'bout we just put Wonder

Woman on your door.

# Thursday's Child Had Far to Go

## Former Vet Commits Suicide

They say it was the war that did him in
how he lost his way somewhere between
every day and camouflage. His guns
lined up in the closet next to his cufflink's

jar with bronzed bullets unused. I still have
his little black book, the one he clutched
like a woman's handbag, too tiny to hold
anything more than a secret or something

       beautiful in the shade of red…

Maybe it was his heart, once obsessed
with love and everything good in the world
now impossible to open, locked shut
with fear someone might peek inside.

His death was not really his choice
though back then there were no whys…
that night before he kissed me goodnight
I saw the enemy in his eyes.

## Mouse Queen

Delayed, is the way your forgiveness
arrives, not through the voice
in my sister's tears or during the Grand
Pas de Deux of the sugar plum fairies,
as we sat together during Nutcracker years,
silent in awe of life and Tchaikovsky.

A backwards walker; you enter
space in patterned grace between
olive trees and parked cars knowing
departures are soon to come. My thumb
turns outward towards the passenger's
side, while you wave me by never
offering a ride.

You are an enigma of narrowing bones
with a decade of stillness between us,
and yet I remember your soft-lit face
and cocktail hours before you left in the middle
of drumbeats so easily lost to rain, even now
as you gleam through martyrdom, your tam-tam
banging all the way down to the doldrums.

**Breached**

Once, for curiosity's sake, I slipped
through the jaws of an incessant talker—
like a creature folding its wings,
I prepared for the moving cavity,
made myself small, minimized
shoulders down, as if sliding
through the birth canal, a journey
to the maw of a chatty marionette.

From the start, a colossal mistake
as removal might have proved tricky,
but I'd read about bugs being swallowed
whole, eight-legged creepers sliding
down throats of sleeping souls
in the midst of fantastical dreams.
Somehow the mindless babble drew

me into a network of web-like words;
aimless prattle expelled with spit;
while her mechanical opening increased
diameters minute by minute until
I was reminded of birth and babies
born breech, entering a world in
backwards order; feet first. Thinking,
how stubborn a child can be, how no

amount of plea undoes the fate
of any willful heart. How high-forceps
are dicey tools but save mothers
from death during delivery, how some
people need heaps of wiggle-room
and catch a buzz from seemingly innocuous
rumors, put their foot in their mouth
endless times a day but never know
how to get out of their own way.

## Tantrums

It's the way your teeth sink
into the pout of your bottom

lip, how they appear
to inflict self-injury

within the swell of skin that rides
high over pearly whites;

your wave of heartache
above veneered anatomy.

I try to bite my tongue
when I say, I hate you, but I'm

thinking, please don't go.

## Willingness to Bare All

Statue in the garden, self-absorbed, placed along
the promenade, though you stand in your archaic
pose, one palm separated from sacred parts
by an unyielding breath, you don't fool me,

I know what you're thinking as camellias grow
close to your silhouette.  Green leaves teetering
nearer every day like intruders who dare
cover exposed parts as if you could alarm

bees with nudity, stun them into a comatose
state from the sheer beauty you possess.
Your almost modesty and the farce of a right hand
covering your loveliness is admirable

as I power wash your breasts, water stabbing
your whiteness clean; every creeping petal pushed
flat into stillness. Beware your stance is alarming
to the eyes of trees who request birds

to defecate as they wing by an unclothed frame.
Still, you are one slab away from being human,
spared the ache of someone cracking your armor
and shattering such sculpted perfection.

## Bad Poem

This is the kind of poem, that wears a low-cut
dress on Sunday afternoons, after a secret jaunt
with her sister's boyfriend, leaving iridescent
stains of lipstick smeared across his fingers
from pages he flipped through unfaithfully,
the words too naughty to resist.

This is the kind of poem, that uses lewd language
hidden in the cleavage of its worn-out
breasts, through a jittering commotion of sounds
you'd rather unhear, as they only leave you
feeling disgusted in a shallow, secondhand kind of way.

This is the kind of poem, that struts around
with no purpose, a guilty pleasure kind of poem
that rubs its vellum skin all over your body,
and you can't scrub it off, no matter how hard
you try, your thumbprints everywhere, like a kid
in the candy store.

This is the kind of poem, that will sleep with you
when no one's looking, on a day you're feeling
especially low, unloved and dejected, and just in case
you begin to think it might a decent poem,
in a bad poem's body, it will tell all your friends
you're a hypocrite, a cheater

in the name of beauty, unfeeling and arrogant,
trying to be something you're not. It will say
things like, 'show me what you're reading,
and I'll tell you who you're sleeping with.'
Because bad poems do that to good people.

**Falling-Out and Over**

Don't speak of last Thursday
at two, the way the Magnolia
looked through the breakability
of our window, its rain-glass
blurring the coldness outside

in. Like you, I have learned
to shield myself from heartache
on days when there are no answers
for reconciliation, because
I'm good at busywork and passing

time, my mind engaged with tonight's
recipe for dinner. It's easier to hope
you'll be sorry in the morning.
Beyond my window the early
stages of tomorrow are unfaltering,

enough to see the start of something
rising again. Even the heart, buried
deep within shields itself from numbness
where the mind relies on reason.
Every season another memory

will surely be lost to indifference.

## A Good Year to Die

Clocks were never meant to lie
facedown on nightstands; evenings
lost to the muffled tick of time—

eclipsed by darkness where she slept
in the nude; her skin brushing
covers dampened from the slow

dripped stain that matched a shade
of broken flesh. She didn't hear him
leaving where footmarks drenched

the stairs to a doorway tightly shut.
No one's sure how she survived,
and most days she doesn't remember a thing.

## Womanizer

He was a weightless cat
that sprang from bed to cradle;
zeroing in on the hard belly
of every girl with breasts
as firm as lemons—

where no pencil kept
within a fold of skin
was fast enough to
scribble time between
the pounce from one to more—

his arrangement, door
to door of scattered leaps
of distance meant and blueness
given, save the sanctity
of climactic bliss, a kiss
with brevity reflected

on his teeth; those lipstick
stains upon his Cheshire
grin, the only damning
proof; a public library
of where and who he'd been.

## Film Stills, On Deceit

I waited, knowing he'd come,
the day forever sepia stained,

corner glued to memory. I don't recall
the hours spent, only the afterward

of silence; the penalty of grieving
half made promises, goodness dethroned,

my mother's voice on the telephone,
some curious comfort when everything

goes awry, the angst of being disloyal,
even the gardenias accusatory

on the table. The scent of gin weighting
the air like some kind of dare each

time he threw back his swig of amnesia.
Unable to raise from the bed, I laid silent,

my soul divided where I laid awake
and stilled from the window's unrelenting glare.

.

## At the Molecular Level

He thought if she held his tears
she might be swayed to mischievous

behavior, increasing the odds of their soon
to be tryst. And the feeling of tenterhooks

an exhausting dilemma, all those butterflies
banging their wings through his horny

stomach. After all, he'd read about mice,
how the males are weepers releasing

pheromones the ladies just can't resist.
But when he cried, she thought his eyes

were bathed in mourning instead of lust,
and her heart became immune

to the thrust of his pelvis for fear
vulnerability gave her an unfair advantage,

something he hadn't planned on.

## Note from Grover

Grover's been taking forty winks in a wooden wagon,
stuffed between Christopher Robin and Paddington Bear,
because he's retired now. Once he swept the floor
from the arm of a young girl, where he'd become
a good companion, a real stickler for paying attention
to tall tales. Before she'd given up on her own
story of love and marriage, sacred vows and unbroken
promises, now left to flounder in loneness, her days
overridden with the guilt of wanting to end all that
needed ending. And she remembered all the moments
he'd add his words, in his own Muppet language.
Those were the times the girl found him
especially charming. She'd ask for his help,

and he'd say things, like, "yes, it is I, your furry blue
taxi driver." Grover understood things like being
frightened by monsters in gloomy closets after mothers
reading, *Where the Wild Things Are.* He was insecure
just like her so he loved the way she wanted
comfort on the nights a half-tipped moon appeared
to be an opening in the inky night, where goblins
and gargoyles might slip through—she'd squeeze
him extra tight and kiss his cherry nose. He was happy
he was made of blue on those days; the perfect
camouflage for blushing. And even though he's been
overlooked for the last few decades, just last night

he heard her weeping when her husband was in
the other room. He tiptoed out of his little oak cart,
crawled under the girl's flannel sheets, whispered
her name in his best Grover voice, and offered
her a sloppy peanut butter and jelly sandwich, following
a bowl of vanilla ice-cream. She cupped him close
to her heart, and in her silly Muppet voice told him
that he'd always be her very best friend.
They shared a glass of chardonnay, commiserated
on life, relationships, and feeling lonely, and decided
being a puppet had been hard on both of them.

## Conman-Duplicitous

She never forgave the nights
he forgot to call, arriving late
from work, the lost hours found
inside his throat during sleep

when names of other women
tattooed on his tongue rolled
off his lips without apology.
Past the midnight trysts, he thought

hidden that broke her body in ways
no one knew. How some mornings
her back ached from the weight
of his breath moving over her

in dreams, the air blued and bruised
from lies when he did his best to love
her. Some days she'd dress for dinner,
wrap a strand of pearls around her neck,

dot her breasts with perfume and parade
around the house in stilettos hoping
a man would ring the bell…
ask her out for a dirty martini, tempt

her to tread the line between faithfulness
and betrayal, until she'd finally give
in, record her rendezvous, play it back
the next time the moon parted the drapes

illuminating her husband's deceptive face.
She'd wake him from a deep slumber,
his heart writhing from the cruel
sound of lust and loathing.

## Sleeping Beauty, Betrayed

It was his teasing kiss that broke
my deathlike slumber and cracked
the malfeasant curse of the wicked
fairy. But no one knows the years

that followed. How he traveled
the breadth of Kingdoms
in search of damsels to feed
his absent heart. A regal

adulterer, semen scattered
throughout the land like crumbs
to birds, paved the way for every
ribbon wearing, unloosed

wanting, breeding machine.
One hundred years of sleeping—
my fair-haired soul untouched,
perfect memories of hypnotic

nights alone on my island without
him. La Belle au Bois dormant
destined to solitude. A life twice
tainted by each enchanted prick.

## Babylon

When I did prison time—
I self-surrendered in exchange
for pink oleanders in my cell.
I bit my tongue to learn
the art of lying. I passed
the days by counting murderers
across the hall and dreamt
of riding my bike through a grove
of trees, the queen of hearts
stuck between the spokes, noisy
keys running over bars. And when
it was just too much to bear, I ate
the flowers instead of food and wrote
the names of my favorite poets
on the wall, and yours was there.

## Detonate

I want to explode
out of death;
be beautiful again.
But I'm a cadaver
alive and swallowed
with pain. Sometimes
I lie on the hollowed
part of the mattress;
a dead embryo
asleep in my bed.
I remember
hearing her lungs
gurgle for long minutes,
while she choked
on swallowed air,
until I could unbend
her to a flattened state
while being eaten alive,
my tongue curled back
from loss of words.
I fear I'll grow mute
by the time I die.
A thing sucked out of air,
morphed into disease.
Because beautiful died
between eleven-
thirty and midnight,
called me there
from an unconscious state
into my
mother's hell and no one
heard a thing.

## The Vibrator

While lounging in the tub, with beads of rain pinging
on the rooftop, and a small vanilla scented candle
moving its flame in sync with the weather
I find myself hypnotized by the subtle rhythm
of external forces, taking me to a far-off place
in what seems a lifetime ago, by the reminder
of a hollowed gift and it's now empty box,
resting on the tub's marble ledge.

No souvenir could be as telling as that silent
case, which once housed your prized possession…
a gift from you to me, the vibrator. And I'm
reminded of the movie, *Splendor in the Grass*
from my teenage days and the melancholy
of feeling alone in the way love can be a place
you live in, unless it becomes your undoing.

I'd never yearned for a make-believe lover,
a fast trip to ecstasy, your laidback donation
supplied when one's body craves another,
and the simple act of loving is easier
from the hand rather than the heart.

I'd go on to evenings without you, frenzied
days between sleep, and still, beautiful
children that happened on at least two
good nights when passion took over
and for this—
you gave me a vibrator

I made you a home, ironed shirts, honored
your father and mother, played homemaker
and wife in the midst of chaos and a companion
never there with a million excuses to my parents
for husbandless evenings spent alone,
midnights by the phone with no call or answer
and for this—

you gave me a vibrator.

I promised till death do us part, in sickness
and in health, and offered the coupling of a heart,
your gardener of blossoming trees, accountant
and chef, accomplisher of tasks large and small
as some would say I gave you my all
and for this—
you gave me a vibrator.

And here, I would say to you now, is the box
that sits bare and unfilled, which needs
no replacements. Here is the case which you
happened to leave while taking the vibrator
upon our divorce which I never questioned
knowing you'd need it—
far more than I.

# Friday's Child Was Loving and Giving

## The Night I Lured Him to Me

*—after Federico Garcia Lorca's: The Unfaithful Housewife*

Then I led him to my chambers
where I dressed myself in petals,
as if the roses needed kissing
upon my breasts where his lips
were lost about my skin.
Though he had a wife, and I a husband
it was only once I told him
that I would betray my
vows, and so he obliged me for the sake
of honor as it would be humiliating
to turn down such a come-on
from a woman twice his age.

His chin quivered when I bit
the toggles of his shirt, and no one
could have imagined the hardness
within him, the roots that took
hold of me and pulled my soul
inside. I told him stories
of young virgins laying on a bed
of hydrangeas naked in the sun,
hoping his mind would see beyond
my age to when I was once young.
I begged his body to seduction
and said, remember me on days
when you are old, and the trees
are leafless beyond your window
when clouds ignore your prayers,
and the sky doesn't listen to your pleas.
Remember me on the day
you are most sad and take comfort
in knowing you brought me joy.
He asked me to kneel beside the bed,

whisper and say his name in songlike
fashion, the way the wind blows soft

on a summer's eve. His hand brushed
across my face and I let my slip fall
below my waist as he held the twilight
in his eyes. The room became a starless
space of darkness where he
told me beautiful things
where we danced on linen
sheets the way angels move
through deathless ghosts, where I
baptized him into my own religion
where he used me, and I used him
while I forgot my wifely ways
where the silkiest flower became
swollen with dew.

## A Mall in California

*(After Reading A Supermarket in California)*

What needs I have for you tonight, Victoria Secret
for I stroll past the naked mannequins, half-dressed
with funnel-shaped breasts and hair of lacquered pearl.

A girl who prays for moonlit nights to angle light
just right and bombard my windowpane with galaxies
of unknown inventory. But you with your aisles full

of thong-back panties and lace-net bras of fleur-de-lis,
I can imagine the husbands' hallelujahs. What plums
with hidden nectars, ripe as teats for nursing babes.

And you, Johnny Depp, I am here a minute past
the dressing rooms. I saw you Victoria Secret.
I saw you placing your mirrors akimbo to the walks,

rose-toned halogens brightening up the ambiance.
Are you my savior? My wingless goddess giving me hope?
I danced in serpentine steps between the cashier

and the husbands needing a centerfold, but I am old,
and my mind is hostage to fantasy. I pass the girls
with robust frames, standing amidst the pendulums

constant tick. The clock whisperer is calling my name.
Where are you going, Victoria Secret? Security is closing
the double-chained door. Which heels are best for this nudity

show? You are the mother of bringing sexy back and arousing
desire from some pitiless sight, my plight a nude desire
where ambition is fueled by fire, and no man can say no

to an unhooked bra. Ah, Victoria, sweet encourager
of support and midnight fallacies, what has become
of the flower-child bohemian mantra, the breathing heart

79

of uninhibited passion, where nothing proves
as beautiful as bosom pressed to skin?

## Orchidmania

Though she could be accused
of orchidelirium, her husband relished
the way she obsessed over the exotic

flowers. Her terrarium of tubers and Venus
slippers where cymbidiums taunted
the voyeur with petals folded

and curled in gleaming arrays
of blushing tones. The neighbors called
her fetish an overt display of sexual

bribery, and no husbands were allowed
to step foot in her hothouse of horticulture
riches. There were days she paraded

near the window, back and forth
she would pace the floor, flora gathered
in her arms. Somewhere she thought

there's a stingless lover with pollen
still dipped on his wings, a flying gigolo
and worshiper of sepals and blooms

she would be his human bandicoot
her obsession a form of madness,
her bedroom, toxic to the point

of asphyxiation.

## If I Should Die before I Wake Remember...

That my life was a long lament
of Saturday sorrows. Weekends
hearing about shock treatments
and forgotten war heroes. Those
are the neglected parts, the sections
I'd overlook when telling you
how it all worked out. I've enjoyed
my grandmother's wisdom and her
walks between broken trees in peach
orchards. I wish I'd saved her windchimes
that would've been a worthy souvenir.
But children don't think of these things
when the gale is making its music.

I cherish my mother's toe shoes
from ballet days and pirouettes
in tulle. And when she died I
realized her life was a beautiful performance
a dabble in the melancholy with black
tears full of mascara falling from the sky.
I could lie and say she wasn't aware
of her complexities, that her burdens
never become mine, yet they did,
and I loved her more for pretending
to be helpless. I'm certain an unseen
strength was sewn into her heart
with a silver needle that left us both
bleeding every time I held her close
enough to feel the fragility of her skin.

At night I hear my father's weeping,
the sound of his feet banging against
the footboard. Once he tried to walk
without me, and I almost lost him
to the vast emptiness that swallows up
a life. I still have his broken teeth,
collectibles he'd like to save, kept

in an ornamental box as if someday
they could be glued back in, as if they
had something left to tell.

I've been blessed with daughters
and sons, their voices filled my head
with dreams of dandelions
and prayers of gratitude that grew
in size and breadth every time they said
my name. They are the poems I've yet
to write as they will become a part of me
no matter what devastation the world
sends my way.

And to my husband, who taught me
to seek the unborn wish, to rise beyond
myself into something wild like milkweed
yet remain soft enough to be a safe
harbor for the most delicate thing.
I'm still learning to understand
the cluster of stars in his eyes;
that trickle of moonbeams from his pockets,
unnerving details that just might prove
he isn't real.

## Wifely Houdini Promise

When my body no longer
feels the rain, forgets the way
to quiver at even the sound
of your voice, loses the strength
to make footprints in freshly
cut lawn, right over left,

left over right, and before
the night we disappear
from the other, vanish without
notice enough to say goodbye
as time can be unforgiving
when death calls your name...

my closet will still be filled
with shoes, neatly displayed
in perfect order, though hollow
inside, if I am the first to go.
Please know, I will be watching
over you, through the skylight,

the dog still laying on my pillow,
my vase of lavender gathered
in a cluster of cut glass, our bedroom
window slightly ajar, a trickle
of stars slipping through,
surrounding you with heaven,

my best pair of Louboutins
missing in the morning.

## In the Order of Loving

Where I am his second wife, and he, my second
husband; let it be said that no first was ever
better than the last as far as we're concerned.

Where once our separate lives became
a quagmire, both of us found in turnaround
positions, each searching for a way

back from another, a bad beginning finding
the other through the journey of seconds.
My first kiss a shudder of something unknown,

a wet peck of puppy love, while the second
involved his tongue and the thrill of leaving
that kind of innocence forever. An unexpected

secret revealed, even to me, until then. So when
we discuss our firsts of things, our litany of once
and agains surpassed by the seconds I wonder

at what point the overfamiliar might seem dull,
how the drudgery of the norm could echo experiences
later abandoned to indifference. I must remember

there is no second without the first, no afterward
before the start, only chance paired with opportunity
providing the opening of an instant that united

each moment of us. How right this calculation
we've found amplified by time, where I pray
somewhere near the end of my life, I will have

remained the latter of two, yet still the one
and only at being my husband's second wife.

## PostScript

In the poem "I Once Loved a Girl" by someone
you once loved, question marks should be replaced
by em dashes in lines 3 through 12.

Please note, the moon was just a device to light
the page on a dark night. There was no mistaking
a willow tree for that slender figure wearing his arms.

Mischief is unwrapped, at least know that.
He carried a bait box for camouflage, but
remained empty in his search; a smokescreen

for boredom was beneath it all. In dreams
he appeared cryptic; some bizarre tactic to draw
you in, though while you slept, he was catching

your breath and saving it for her. She was a dullard
in flowerlike form as beauty was his weakness.
There is no final stanza for the poem he wrote.

No extent of examination will explain these
oversights except the way you misinterpreted
his poems.

## Red Cape for Sale

Veil bright as lipstick
once worn by the lone girl
seeking her grandmother's
love. Often mistaken for virtue
this cloak screams, SAVE ME,
to heroes and wolves. Could
prove interesting to those
who like to wander through
woods picking begonias.
A promised escapade
awaits you with a happy ending
or closetful of lumberjacks
with good intentions. Please
only reply to this ad if you
enjoy being hoodwinked
and labeled as the innocent
victim. Practice saying things
like, "Oh my, what big eyes
you have" and "Nana you look
so strange!" The art of appearing
surprised is equally important
if this cape is used to its full
potential.  If you no longer visit
relatives or elderly folk or you
object to a tear in the lining
from a few undisclosed
mishaps you need not apply. Also
interested in trades; poison apples,
red shoes, an emperors new suit.

## Pheromones

Ah, how I wanted to be you,
your beauty was magnificent.
He embraced your frail being
as though you might tear
if not handled with most delicate precision
fastening his arms around you,
beginning his love-making ritual,

and the world was nonexistent
yet, I was there, a voyeur in the midst
of such beautiful splendor.
How could I resist the engagement?
Thoughts went stirring through my head,
how he kissed your moist mouth and loved you
in a way of losing himself,

as for a time disappearing
during the rapture…
wearing you for his clothes,
his warmth, and pleasure.
Ah, how I wanted to be you,
to feel the intensity of his passion
the glow of such wantonness
reveling in the conquest.

Though you acted so complacent
so unaffected by it all, this
seeming to stir him even more,
and I a mere onlooker you never saw
making him gloat with pride as he had
his way with you in the most brilliant moment
as he demonstrated such finesse
with speed and accuracy all the while
achieving his goal.

Ah, flower, to be loved by such a bee.

## Boudoirs of Lavender Oil

Between an eyelid of light, eclipsed
by a lavender moon, the undressed fellatrix
splays above a dovetailed fitted

counterpane, in oily nudeness, curved
to womblike grace after erratic rounds
of punishing-love. Her boudoir's a room

of whispers and hums while he comes
to a Venus girl's wicking massage. Aromatherapy
and Kama-Sutra-evenings, where she plays

his flute, shifts to the lilac echo of muted
moans over cylindrical motion, where nothingness
groans and draws in the scent of violet

skin; a flowering explosion so abundant
within, she imagines channeling life
from the downing swallow, all the way

to the impregnation of fallopian tubes.

## Introduction to Aromatherapy

So, you'd hope for the essential oil,
someone devoid of synthetic ingredients;
their jojoba blend, an aphrodisiac of exfoliates
rubbing off your excess layers, leaving you
distilled to feminine absoluteness. Oh, to be
an Eve-like girl with unlimited beauty. But
no one promised he'd inhale your loveliness,
breathe in your hydrosols and herbs. He was
a loather of lungs, a eucalyptus freak. And though
you practiced your rigorous magic, nothing
could prepare you for the man who refused
to inhale. You and your unprovable scent,
Sweet Birch and Wintergreen child
naive to the etymology of love, the dusting
of fragrance in unmentionable places,
there is no hope for lemongrass madness
unless there is steam or aerial flight.

**When I Think of You**

Our days were lost to dwellings
made of fingers instead of rooms,

at night I laid inside your palm
my legs nimble as wedding

flowers. When you whispered
my name, your voice became

a midnight drink, the arch
of your hand an upturned

home of hallowed bones and ecstasy.

## Jaded Housewife Watches Bare-Chested Workman

She leers as he places rebar in perfect
angles, corners joined with precision,
she's in awe of his movement, a flawless
syncopation from one step to the next.
She forgets about the laundry, mealtime
at eight, her children waiting for a ride;

while they stand alone and count the minutes
as if she'll be there soon, unaware their
mother's being swooned, a violation
of the heart, a whim—a lark, a sin?
She remembers being young without
a care, delicious as a pear that waded

from the lowest branch easy in sun.
She's become an aging wife, with
would-be lovers and a fantasy life,
a worn-down woman in a body once
blessed, now beaten by time's

too-critical chime, a devoted thinker
of humble views, a willing muse who
dreams of accidental trysts before
the evening's morphed to grocery lists.
She longs for days when her body
was craved in erotic ways, tender

as the whoosh of wind through hair—
everywhere the holy joy of freedom,
and half-kept promises never met,
her options open beyond the now
of endless stress, past all caution
care and grace, a onetime urge,

to be unchaste.

## Hiatus

We're on a tiny sojourn from our midnight
hour; the little deaths that invade our bed
on what used to be a regular basis,

leaving two bodies comatose, after a whirling
array of flesh on bone. Tonight, he rests his glass
half empty, beside mine, yet alone on the night

stand, bleeding condensation through lukewarm air.
We're not really here nor there but lost somewhere
within, and I bemoan then grin as he reaches

for my hand unknowing where fingers will land,
hoping this might just be the end of our brooding,
meditative phase. I pray he doesn't feel

too parched and go for a swig from the glass
nearest him, as I've dropped my contacts inside
the rim, and if he swallows my lenses I won't be

able to see the thirst in his eyes.

## Insert the Current Date and Time

If you ever leave me, blame
it on the way I said your name;

the irritation that came with being
sweet when loving has exhausted

the soul from too many losses. My self-
preserving vigilance anointed to you,

as aging days accrue. If you ever leave
me, open the windows to the gusty

dark. Let the wind yowl through
the room to the sound of a downpour,

an unstoppable gale that drowns
the muffled song of any skylark that sings

for you. Within this weighted farewell
I carry the burden or a hidden sin

removing virtue, fearing the unbearable
silence of goodbye, inaudible as feathers

of a flying thing in rain.

**Saturday Chores**

While deadheading lavender
roses in the backyard on a Saturday
afternoon, with the weather sending
its searing heat upon my semi-tanned
skin; wearing a Chanel bikini, the top
tied with a modest string in a supple
bow somewhere across the middle
of my back, I'm thinking I must
look good in a Martha Stewart
goes beachy kind of way, outside
in the midday heat, trimming down
the dying petals. When I could be
baking on my forties-style lounge
chair, sipping strawberry daiquiris,
instead of doing the hard labor
of clipping the blooms off prickly
stems swaying in the ninety-degree
breeze; my tousled hair rustling
over semi-exposed breasts. And I wonder
why no one's outside to notice
my gardening skills as I must
look spectacular yet formidable
to hummingbirds and bees, disrupting
their day with an early execution
of flowers; the decapitation expert
that I am, and it occurs to me that I should
perhaps go topless, pretend I'm on the French
Rivera, say "Bonjour garçon" to the cabana
boy who's just opening the garden gate,
so I might feel naughty, as though
I'm eighteen again, because I never
did anything like that, even then.

# Saturday's Child Worked Hard for a Living

## For All the Places We Used to Be

We used to ride horses across the hillside.
You leading the way through a sea
of ivy, as though there was a sacred place
to be, rebels beyond our means or just
our mothers' silver dinner bell.

We used to meet by the old picket fence.
One white line separating me from you
until one of us took the risk of a sliver.
A good reason to light a match, our patch
of skin to skin, one thin drop of blood
for sisterhood.

We used to sit in a circle, on an old
wooden floor, one candle lit to summon
the spirits, your hand in mine, a half-
opened door, trusting the light would save us,
our pockets full of incense and empty wrappers.

We used to hold a mirror in the dark
and whisper a name against the glass,
Hark! As if our voice could travel past
time, survive the curse of Mary Worth,
the two of us praying we'd make it out alive.
Each of us vowing to save the other.

We used to sit on the piano bench
in the summer's heat, wearing pinafores
over bony knees, your fingers striking ivory
keys as I flipped through the pages keeping
up with your endless song
until one day it was only me.

## An Orchid's Life

You were an orchid for a while
thriving in the Black Sea.
You aren't really a flower anymore
beneath your soft perfumed scent.
Tenderness once flowed in your warm silk-petal skin,
but those were days when your upswept lips
began every morning.
When you were still a child, unknowing, unaware,
pretending you'd never grow old.

Who could prepare you?
Your father did his best, your mother too.
It's not their fault; you blame them though,
that's your selfish part.
The part that rejects the truth, unwilling to accept
what needs accepting. Don't rely on anything.
Who's in charge here anyway?
They did you a favor, leaving early,
showing you life moves fast, changes quickly.

And now you see the fragileness, kissing moist leaves
of the ones you call your own.
The seeds you grew from darkness.
They will blame you too, say you let them down,
left earlier than you should have.
Someday when they're no longer flowers,
when they remember being young
wondering how they grew old—
If they've loved you enough.

**The Blue Rosary**

Little Lucy wanted to be a nun.
Sometimes she would safety pin the corners of a thin black blanket
around her neck. Her mother said she looked more like a superhero

than a nun. Lucy didn't believe in superheroes, but she believed in nuns.
At night she hung a rosary from the chandelier and watched it swing
like a pendulum ricocheting bursts of light like a kaleidoscope around her room.

She lined her dolls in long rows and placed each hand upon the next until they
made what appeared to be a chain of babies flat upon the floor. Lucy's dolls
had no parents, but they had each other.

Lucy's father died when she was 8. If Lucy could have believed
in superheroes, she would have believed in him,
but superheroes aren't supposed to die.

After Lucy's father died, the nuns brought a blue rosary along
with a handwritten note her mother saved, saying how sorry they were.
When Lucy was 18, she went away to school.

She took the rosary and her collection of dolls, but her mother
made her leave the blanket, which by then was full of holes.
Lucy's roommate Kathy was a childhood friend. Her father had died too.

On lonely nights when they missed being at home, they would hold hands
to fall asleep. They had no father but they had each other.
Kathy knew Lucy's father had committed suicide.

Lucy's mother said her father had died in a bad accident.
One night when Lucy and Kathy were holding hands, trying to fall asleep,
Kathy said she was sorry that Lucy had lost her father to suicide.

She told Lucy that her mother read it in the paper, and everyone felt badly.
Lucy wondered why her mother had lied and if she would die in a bad
accident too. Years went by, and Lucy met a man she fell in love with.

Her mother said he had the same eyes as her father. Some days
Lucy wanted to be a nun so she could feel closer to heaven.
Lucy's mother said heaven looked like her father's eyes.

Once, the nuns told Lucy they were married to Jesus.
Lucy thought Jesus might be a superhero, but she couldn't prove it.
One day, Lucy found the note the nuns wrote after her father died.

It was in her mother's nightstand drawer along with a picture
of her father, but his eyes were full of sorrow instead of heaven.
Lucy's mother died in a 'bad accident' too, so Lucy buried her with the blue

rosary and black cape. She held her husband's hand and told him
as long as they were together, they would never lie, and their eyes
would always be full of heaven instead of sorrow.

They had no parents, but they had each other.

## Scrutinizing the Nun's Story

The day I watched the Nun's Story,
I imagined myself as Audrey Hepburn.
My face in the mirror, I draped a snowy
scarf around my neck, wore my brother's

dark cape backwards, my hands folded
for prayer. I placed my father's
dowry (a few dollars stolen from his wallet),
inside my pocket,

my suitcase packed beside me
for a life's excursion containing no
possessions save a handful of memories
stilled within and ready for release

as soon as my feet passed over
the threshold of the rectory. And when
called to cut my hair, I could hear myself
saying, 'send the remnants

to grandma who will weave a lovely
macramé out of anything.' In my heart,
I would quell the desire to be fulfilled—
to put another's dreams before my own

yet, I'd felt unworthy in my moment of dreaming
about borders not ready to cross.
So, I returned my brother's black cape
and stroked my almost cut curls,

and thought what a disappointment
I would have been to my mother
had I ever attempted such holiness.

## Things I Remembered After You Died

A guiding light above your head,
like a pearlescent bubble
that held all the secrets of the universe.

A sculpture misplaced among the years;
like someone who might have loved me,
or just a statue lost among gardenias.

A room of yellow on days you fell between
the halfway feeling of being in the middle—
a type of existing without committal.

A TV with rabbit ears, which became
your mantra in darkness, when insomnia
set into aloneness amplified.

A girl who loved your wicker chair,
the one you painted, where you used
to sing, but no one heard a thing.

A radio in a blue Ford station wagon,
your lit cigarette wafting through
clouds, even now, long after you've died.

## Keep Me This Night

We used to drive on Sunday afternoons
in her red convertible, twisting over the windy

path of Lombard street, her hair wrapped
tight in a white chiffon scarf, two sashes

whipping in air, the two of us there in her 56
Thunderbird. One of those old-fashioned

hardtops we'd tie up from the garage
ceiling with a harness my daddy rigged.

I'd watch it sway, suspended like a chandelier
until our next ride. Those were the days

when childhood lied; my mother
requesting company, and I'd sit outside

her pink room mesmerized by femininity
as she'd attach one eyelash at a time.

Spinnerets of long silk threads weaving
around brown eyes that gleamed at everything

until the day she died when we sold her T-bird,
gave away her fancy things and I was told

now you must learn what it means, to be strong.

## A Day in the Life

She said, "you can't chew gum in Thailand,"
when I was eight, wearing pale oxfords with polished

laces, artificial roses strung behind scrubbed ears;
asked to place that unacceptable thing in my mouth

on the chalkboard, before of a roomful of uniformed girls.
If only I were home gazing out the window of my little pink

house, the ice cream truck whizzing by, my old dog
laying under the table waiting for half-chewed scramble

eggs in the same spot where I sat playing mahjong with my best
friend, Ann. We used to sneak girly magazines from her father's

bedroom, barely opening them for fear of punishment
as if the nuns would somehow find out. The same nuns

who gave me a blue crystal rosary when my father died.
All I can remember was sitting together for hours

in his old Ford wagon listening to Elvis, thinking we'd both
live forever. I used to tell him, my mother was so beautiful

I'd dream of swinging on her eyelashes, and he
always smiled and said, he had that dream too.

## Child in the Distance

I want to remember the days
of being young. Of being
the same height as my mother's knees.

Of carrying a tub of fruit inside
from the orchard while the sunlight
drown the fallen leaves in gold,

and everyone I loved waiting
at the kitchen table, my father
in his fiddleback chair, holding

a gin and tonic and a lit cigarette.
But those aren't memories anymore;
they're tiny pages scribbled

in an old diary, after the war,
tucked beside the rules of etiquette
like treasured bibelots. Still,

if I try hard enough to recall the feeling
of being a child, it was for an instant,
a flicker of whimsy; a barrel

of uneaten fruit, the tenderness
of handpicked apple blossoms
pressed against my chest.

## Ode to You

Were I to see you now, I'd speak
of Convent days when we were
young, when you would tease
thin fingers through my hair
and sweep my neck with gardenia
leaves so I could feel the touch
of wings upon my skin. I want
to begin again, having you here

to see me all grown up after
a womb blessed with children,
and the weddings of two husbands.
I'd love to smell your vanilla skin
and touch your feathered hair,
the scent of candles in the air—

Dan Fogleberg echoing through
our walls, it was nineteen-seventy-five,
and you were still alive with hope
as sweet as April rain. Remember
when the first storm came? Your mother
called you home that year. I heard
that you went mad, your light
eclipsed before I ever had a chance

to say how beautiful you were.
Were I to see you now I'd speak
of school days in the garden
where the nuns would watch us play.
We were the same as one when
we were young, and that time you said
you loved me, when I turned away
in silence because I couldn't
stand to know.

## Calibrating a Childhood Musing

I have my father's old Winchester
unloaded and stowed in a tall Chinese
vase beside my nightstand. Even
though it's an odd souvenir
from my childhood, it helps me sleep
in the event, there's an intruder.
Though it couldn't save me, I imagine
myself with my fingers on the trigger,
half-cocked and ready to fire. It's almost
like having him there.
Except it isn't.

When I was little, he used to take me
hunting. We'd bring broken-necked
birds home to my mother who'd pluck them
bare and prepare them for our Sunday's
feast. I used to float his duck decoys
into my wading pool and watch them
glide back and forth in the sunlight.
It was almost like having wildfowl
take a dip in the water with me.
Except it wasn't.

Sometimes I think it was strange
that my mother allowed him to take me
on those trips, surrounded by men
with guns, shooting beautiful winged
things right out of the sky. Once he went
without me and brought home a live
jackrabbit stuffed in his pocket,
like a consolation prize for not going.
Except it wasn't.

I've thought about selling that rifle now
and then, wondered how much it would be
worth if I ever had the nerve to get rid
of it. But there's something sacred about

that old gun. The memory of how we used
to walk through the cattails, how he'd point
to the wide-open sky and say, watch this,
and a flurry of wings would spiral down
through clouds; like a wounded angel
falling from heaven.
Except it wasn't.

## Damages

Sometimes we'd sit around the kitchen
table drinking our milk and eating snap

peas with our flank steak dressed
in truffle mushroom sauce,

discussing wrongdoings between
bites of popovers. This was no place

for tall tales or hilarity. This was
the kind of talk that ate through

dreams like a beetle on a willow
leaf. Legal jargon thrown about

between sips of purity and well-
done beef, and as I recall one debate

about a girl's puppy who gnawed through
a pair of her father's brand-new Loafers…

how after weeks of bad behavior,
he told his daughter to

"take that dog to the mustard fields
and shoot him with my rifle—"

how she unlocked the gun, and shot
herself instead. I never could manage

a worthy comment. I just sat
in silence and pondered the penalty

of refusing to polish my father's shoes.

## Liftboy

There's always the morning after
the elevator dream. The one where
no one's there to squeeze your hand
to grab you back from the freefalling
rope-less shaft that's moving
at umpteen speed, yet somehow
you've managed to get on and down
you go like a bird clipped wingless,

to an unknown mystery of a place
that remains unreachable no matter how
often you slip through this conundrum
or sleep induced coma. And that elevator
is as infinite as your first boyfriend's kiss
before you told him, you weren't that kind
of girl. Now, couldn't you just weep
remembering how he swore he wasn't

going to try anything naughtier than you
had in mind?! And it was all up to your good
judgment to call things off, hold back
the roving fingers over your breasts; your heart
racing to the heat of Electric Light Orchestra,
you having to pull out of your very own being
in order to halt all wildness flaring inside.
There's always been the morning after

the elevator dream when you wake up in bed
and thank God you're alive only to wonder
with all your years of doing the right thing
why are you plagued with such a heinous dream?
And where's that little asshole now with his pushy
lips and tongue, who gave you your first
introduction to guilt, who taught your heart
suspicion before you'd gone too far, your
first encounter with your fear of falling.

## Angie's Garden

I could say the room was yellow
with a trace of gangrene,
or how skilled I became at knotting
strings to hospice gowns so the old
man in room 203 couldn't get
sneak peeks as we paced corridors,
wheeling IV's, like her make-believe
lover whose only mission was giving
sustenance in a one-way relationship.

I could say she annoyed me most
of the time by barking my name with
constant complaints about nagging
nurses and Dixie-cup pills or Mary
Poppins' smiles. That no spoonful
of sugar was helping the crisis,
allaying fears of an old woman
dying in blue slippers.

I could say we pondered some last
minute facts or the splendor of
mountains with overrun trees
as she stared through her window
when daylight seeped in, despite
the shade's half shut position
obstructing her view like a tempting sin.

Yet what we discussed was the fate
of her chickens who lived in the garden
of her abandoned home, who seldom laid
eggs, but feathered the lawn and hid
from the fox when left on their own,
and the unfortunate day they escaped
from the pen; dodging the truth
of those ill-fated chickens, long since dead—

so many things were better unsaid.

## A Few Concessions

I swear I'll cleanse my mouth with ivory soap
for the mention of words like fart and other
awfully nasty things, including unspoken wickedness.

I'll brush my teeth after every meal, string floss
through molars though it hurts to stretch my lips
in lengths of long arrows, for a flawless smile.

I vow to tidy nails, buffed and polished
to beautiful shades of nudeness, curls stroked
one hundred times, till amber silk blends

on perfumed shoulders, twice dabbed with Shalimar.
I'll honor house rules for immaculate underwear
lest I get killed by a drunk moron in a red Corvette.

I'll down the wellness of eight glasses of water,
without a burp, gobble an apple a day, skin and all,
twist the stem to breaking then fancy a foolish wish,

undisclosed for fear of jinxing it. I'll pace the floor
in ballet-flats; man-shoes, the suitable choice
for work, though they look absurd with this not too tight

pencil pressed skirt, double hemmed. Yes, yes, yes!
I'll abide by your annoying litany of orders, hold fast
to strict requests, when all I really want is a moment

you might reappear in your most furious pose
arms akimbo, eyes on fire with tiny yellow flames,
mouth pursed as you bellow in a livid voice,

the one I've always hated, just to hear you scream
my name, the way you used to, for doing it all wrong.

## Ritual Regarding Nakedness

After saying goodnight to him,
we slip into the pale creaminess of our bed—
lying beside him, skin undressed
I wait for his hand to cup my breast.

I'm not thinking of being twenty again,
or the first time I made love to a man
and experienced the sorrow that came
before cigarettes and consolation.

I'm not thinking of a flawless face
or how I'll look when I wake in the morning
with the wren perched on the sill,
the two of us still braided together.

I'm not thinking of our candlelit hour
requiring perfection anymore,
or consideration for the critical eye
that held me hostage through youthful years.

I'm thinking, how do I get through
the days without the feeling of skin
placed in the home of his palm?
So I wait for the usual darkness

to possess us. The only place we
wear each other's flesh.

## Meet Me in the Countryside

When you arrive, I'll be waiting near the gate,
dressed in my best black dress, silk stockings,
and high stacked heels. My handbag halfway
open, one Hermes scarf spilling out of the corner

bubbling in waves from the summer's wind
with a flower in my hair. It will be a rose,
peach and white, with one leaf cupping
the rim of my ear. Pearls will hang, knotted

falling through the cleavage of my heart-
shaped neckline. One earring will jangle back
and forth when I nod my head, as though I'm
amused with the person to my right.

He'll be carrying on and on about this
and that. A touch of Fracas will be dabbed
behind my knees, as tuberose is my favorite
perfume. My arms will be dusted with specks

of silver, like a flickering rain of bright
stars all the way to the tips of my stem-long
fingers. You'll know it's me by my amusing
laugh, the kind of sound, so boastful it nears

the realm of eternal happiness as if a cluster
of butterflies might be released each time
I part my lips, so full of heaven colors
will halo the air with every breath. *Oh,*

you'll say, *how peculiar she is, how peculiar
and strange.* And I will see you there, so fantastical
drunk on faith and love, your eyes enchanted
with what you'd hope to be true. Turn around

when you see me, step back on the train. Nothing
will be more than that very first moment.

So much better to wonder what might have been.
A prelude to ecstasy is all that I ask.

## The Butterfly Room

With a view of the ceiling, its limits exposed
as I lie on my back, both feet harnessed
in flat-bottomed stirrups, I ride along

the table in a horseless room, sliding myself
through an unknown crossing—this ready
position for silver tools and scalpels;

his magnifying light at the mouth
of my womb where only sacred things
are meant to happen. Please forgive

me, my hands are cold, and I flinch through
an awkward smile at the bald-headed
doctor between my knees, telling me

to think pleasant thoughts while he reviews
this place of origin, hollowed now, embryo
free. This is the transformation zone,

and I think, yes, a conversion of sorts;
the metamorphic clock is ticking,
but I remember the fluttering of baby

wings inside me, where all that grows
is indefinable before results are in. He scrapes
my walls thin for malignant-matter, the sound

of clatter from scissors and a knife like a stiletto
in my heart. I hope I was a good wife, mother,
and daughter, then the rush of water,

his hands baptized clean. I'm told to wait
the verdict will soon be in, and I take solace
in this nameless journey before we know

what birthed unseen.

## Shopping with My Grandmother

I shouldn't have seen
you leaving the store
with that fur jacket tucked
under your arm. I was
only a kid, and you guessed
your secret was safe with me
as you turned down the aisle
in the 3rd street mall. It's
been over forty years,
and even now I wonder
how you had the nerve
to undress that mannequin
and maneuver your way
through the parking lot with
such finesse. I might have
said something to the store-
keeper, but my grandmother
was trying on coats and admiring
herself in the mirror,
and you gloated with such
pleasure it gave me a shudder
to think how cold you must have been
to thieve a coat right in front of me,
and that dummy looked so much
better naked anyway.

## To the Man Who Ran Over My Cat

You were to blame for the death
on the road, the roaring cry,
and wild tears of a small child.
You with your guilty eyes
filled with dew. That cat and I
were simpatico souls.
What were you thinking,
you cat killer you? You
with your slow wheel that tortured
my rag-doll friend who slept
curved to the s of my eight-
year-old back. And the way
my mother absolved your sin,
as if that cat was somehow
to blame. I remember the roll
of her radiant purr, the meow,
and milk on a sandy pink tongue.
After all these years, when the engine
rumbles, I want you to know,
though I forgive you, I miss
my cat, and the grace of my mother
who kept me in line and taught
me the art of empathy.

But the Child That Was Born
on the Sabbath Day,
Was Fair and Wise
and Good and Gay.

## Epitaph for the Beloved

How small we are in the midnight hour
nameless yet forever blessed by moonlight—
lost through shadows of eternal homelessness.

How vulnerable to the greatness within clouds
above the hovering hands of heaven, innumerable
wayfarers; bystanders between stars

and mortal chaos, where no lone prayer goes
unanswered, where numberless await the grace
that powers love, past breath and living through death.

How once the hours lingered their nimbus of time
when we were young lest the future would never
come; impatient children unaware of intervening

distance while everyday nearing the keeper
of souls. Where true holiness must surely be,
where the everlasting unravels this mystery,

where soon we will meet at the right hand
of God, in lightness without dark, vast
as the breadth of a merciful heart.

## Make Believe

If she were a poet, she would know the way of rivers,
the easiness of dawdling near the stream,
and finding the sun in the reflection of a penny
once tucked neatly inside a leather shoe
found among the roses weighted with dew—

If she were a poet, she would know the sound
of poltergeist eking through the attic with voices
capable of separating clapboards, the way rain
warps the evenness of wood, she would know
beyond is never far but undeniably, misunderstood—

If she were a poet, she would undress him
with her tongue, one breath at a time with little
prayers blown around the moon and back
again, spinning her halo of wellbeing; a seduction
from midnight to noon, she'd be as foolish as a wish
and the dish that ran away with the spoon.

## For Bette and All Our Sad Afternoons Together

*Fasten your seatbelts, it's going to be a bumpy ride*

Mademoiselle, you should know that I adored you
in all things, Black and White. Your long fingers
and cigarette holders, your quirky voice, a mix

of tobacco and vanilla to the ear of this admirer.
Your fearless portrayals and bitch performances
are inspirational to any outcast Jezebel.

And if melancholy could override any notion
of light from now to the end of time, let it be said,
that one glance from you could force a heart

to weeping. I'd love to offer you an Angostura
Bitters–soaked sugar cube over your favorite
champagne. We could walk into the Coconut

Grove, arm in arm. You with your Hollywood
charm and me with my All This and Heaven Too
love for you. And if anyone dare interrupt our

soiree, we'd just say how we'd love to hug
them, but we just washed our hair.

## A Dancer's Guide to Life and Love

In first position

Your legs are paralyzed
unsure which path will lead you
anywhere better than where you are

In second position

Your body reveals,
opens to chance and possibilities;
a daily dose of barre keeps you alive

In third position

You think maybe a song
will get you there, though your pink
slippers are holding fast heel to toe

In fourth position

You notice the air—
it becomes your lover, your dream
of pirouetting though infinite space

In fifth position

You're lost to heartache,
you've misplaced your soul
to the devil instead of grace

In sixth position

You're more aware,
feet aligned to the hardwood floor,
you're a stoic mnemonic device

In seventh position

You're ready again
you fish-dive into the arms of another
a hopelessly doomed Odette

## Dead Mouse in the Garden

For the tiny mouse, motionless,
under the olive tree, shaded

by a fertile umbrella of green,
lying dormant for the past week.

Today, I'll hold your downy
carcass and place it gently

within a cardboard coffin.
Then I'll dig a shallow grave

somewhere between here
and your path to heaven. I'll crown

the earth with an amber garland
of roses above your resting spot.

Please know that you were loved
if only in the moment I gave up

this cherished shoebox marked
with a designer insignia that housed

a perfect pair of never-worn pumps.
Tomorrow I will bury these shoes—

for they are forever ruined, covered
with grass stains, as I wear them

hallowing your new home
in the garden. It is only right.

## San Francisco to September

Come September, when I reach
my zenith, the atmosphere a petal
pink of blur, when seaplanes
bathe their bellies near the shores

of Tiburon, when your heat bleeds
gold across my garden's floor in search
of fuchsias with their pendulum bell
that creep about the jardinières—

come September, when botanical
lovers unite beneath my San Francisco
air, my Indian summer awaits you
where, if only once a year you'll

find thirty days of splendor. Come
September! Bring your finger fog
where the weather holds its tears,
my Golden Gate suspended over

up-swells spraying legs of travelers
seeking sights beyond their windowpane,
umbrellas left behind in disrepair—
a spray of flowers in their hair.

## Troubleshooting the Sun

I was thinking about the Sun and how it was born
over 4.5 billion years ago, and is expected to endure
4.5 billion more, which seems like a lengthy while
unless you do your calculations in human math.

Then the Sun is having a midlife crisis with one foot
already in the grave. In fact, it's about time for a black
balloon party announcing half an existence already
passed and the best days sure to follow. With more

yesteryears than tomorrows, not that any of us will
be around to find out, but it seems significant to me
being at a halfway point myself. I think we should
celebrate the Sun's midway mark; after all, he's the most

significant celestial body in the solar system. We should
give thanks for stellar glory, pay tribute to nuclear
fusion and astronomical units, declare a holiday of sorts
in honor of sacrificing his younger self for the betterment

of mankind. I mean I know he's only one of over 100
billion stars, but without him, the earth is doomed.
And maybe the Sun is getting damn tired of his thankless
job, spinning on axis every 26 days, programming

unwilling insomniacs with patterns of sleep, and the ongoing
chore of defining Winter from Spring, Summer from Fall,
the exhausting task of keeping his amber light just out
of reach, maintaining order in the midst of chaos

managing all this alone through his golden fever, a life
of solitude and aurora borealis nights, no one there
to stroke his hotness, gaze through his ultraviolet
glow, after long years of corona burning brilliance,

until he implodes from total burnout; the world left iced
over in deadly shadows, suffering through a grisly

death. I fear the Sun's elderly creep and dwindling rule.
The aging process taking a toll on his underappreciated

powers. I dread his soon-to-be red giant phase, exposing
the Earth to a rickety fate, swallowing us whole,
resentful of his once almighty role, putting an end
to our earthly existence; knowing his days are numbered,

sick of being taken for granted and not properly valued,
too much expected for fiery radiance, devoid
of supernatural sway, just another one among us,
not immune to dying and certainly never a God.

## There are Those Who Wait for the Dark

I want to tell you, the moonlight knows your name
which keeps me from forgetting mine, and even
the sunniest morning will never be

as forgiving as your arms in the darkness,
safe as a mother's eyes, before she falls
to an endless sleep. Because I've watched

you sleep, not for a minute but for a hundred
minutes and then a hundred more, and every time
I tried to look away I felt your kindness so deep

within my veins, it was like an open door
that pulled me right inside the room of you—
where I saw my name inscribed above a skein

of stars that beat with the pulse of your body,
an electric surge that rose beyond the familiar
into a hypnotic yet unbound force, daunting

as my belief in God, both tempting and devastating
at the same time, my heart a silhouette searching
past its shadow, your heart so bright there's no

shadow to be found, only light—
the backdrop of everything, the collision of wingless
angels unlost to the thought of love, of placing

your skin against mine, of holding my body to yours,
of saying my voice is our voice, of never being
without purpose—

I want to tell you, the moonlight knows your name,
sees your goodness, hears your prayers,
opens the rivers and whispers through the eucalyptus

trees over the scent of lavender roses in the garden,

and a thousand dandelions growing in tears
from the graveyard where our loved ones slumber

beyond all sadness and joy that can't even
be imagined yet sacred and merciful as this love
that unites us, me and you, you and me,

together, this union, this blending of souls,
this gathering of empathy, this rapture untamed
as the sound of wild horses on their way

to the badlands, our window so full of light,
so bursting with saints on glass, broken
and unbroken, real and unreal, your hand a place

I can walk into, your words a sentence I carry
in my mouth, I want to tell you,
the moonlight knows your name.

Carol Lynn Stevenson Grellas lives in the Sierra Foothills. She studied at Santa Clara University, where she was an English major. She is a nine-time Pushcart nominee and a seven-time Best of the Net nominee. In 2012 she was the winner of the Red Ochre Chapbook Contest, with her manuscript, *Before I Go to Sleep.* She is the author of numerous books and has had hundreds of poems published in print journals and online, including *War, Literature and the Arts,* and *The Yale Journal of Humanities in Medicine.* In 2018 her poem "A Mall in California" took 2nd place for the Jack Kerouac Poetry Prize. Her work has appeared in international publications as well as several anthologies across the U.S. In 2019 her chapbook *An Ode to Hope in the Midst of Pandemonium* was an Eric Hoffer Book Award finalist. She has been the featured poet at countless venues as well as the guest speaker at the California Writer's Club. She is the Editor-in-Chief for *The Orchards Poetry Journal* and Co-Editor-in-Chief for the *Tule Review.* She is a member of the Sacramento Poetry Center Board of Directors, Saratoga Author's Hall of Fame and has been a "visiting professor" at UC Davis. According to family lore, she is a direct descendant of Robert Louis Stevenson.

www.ingramcontent.com/pod-product-compliance
Lightning Source LLC
Chambersburg PA
CBHW021147090426
42740CB00008B/983

*9781635349566*